WHO WOULD WIN?

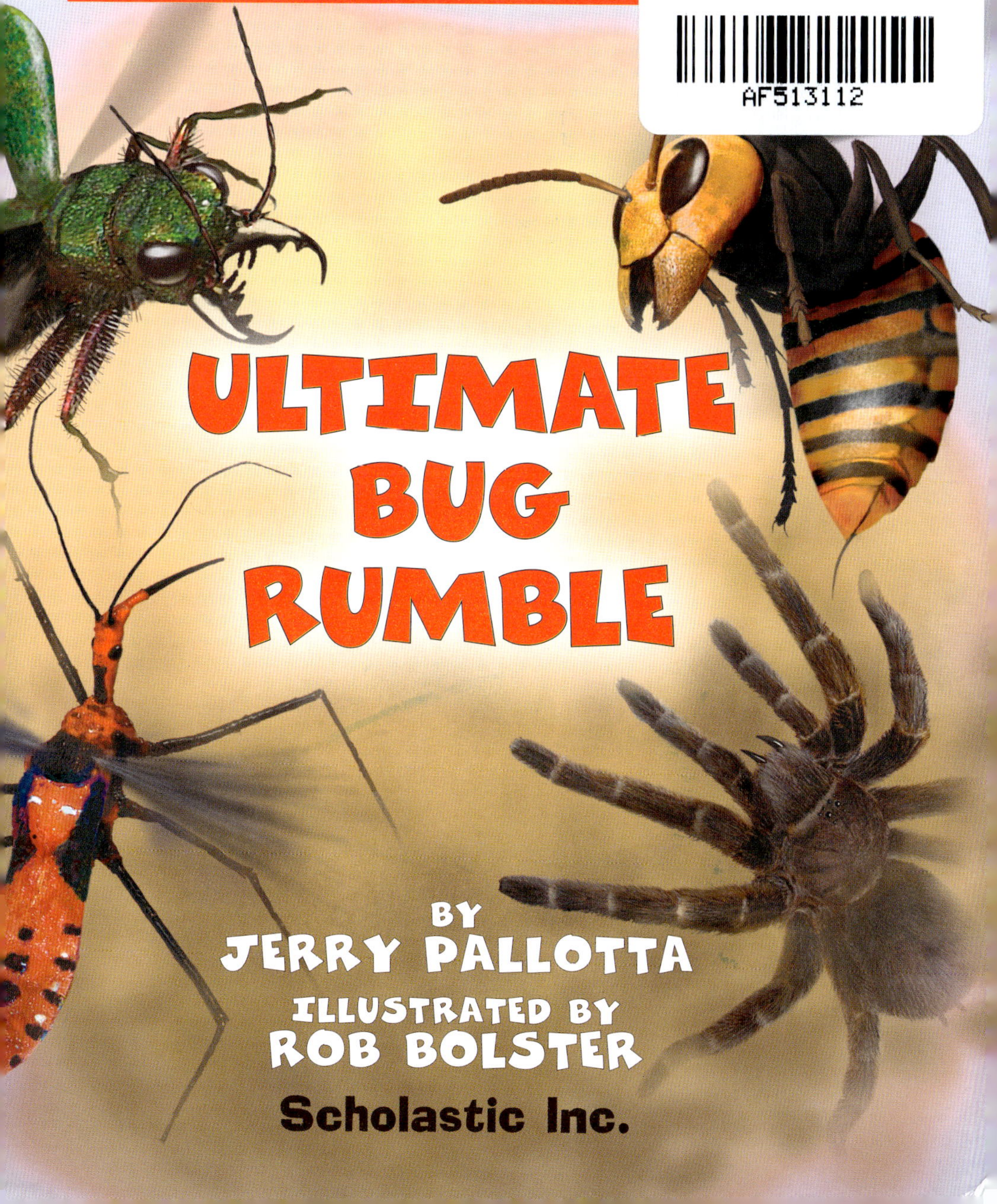

ULTIMATE BUG RUMBLE

BY
JERRY PALLOTTA
ILLUSTRATED BY
ROB BOLSTER

Scholastic Inc.

Thank you for the lift—Sheila, Jill, Nancy, Janet, Ellen, Jane, Christine, Eileen, and Liz
—J.P.

To David.
—R.B.

ISBN 978-93-5471-161-9

10 9 8 7 6 5 4 3 2 1 20 21 22 23 24

This reprint edition : September 2024
Printed in India at : VK Global Digital Private Limited

No one knows why it happened, but sixteen bugs and insects just showed up for a bracketed contest. The rules are simple. If you lose, you are out of the tournament. Who will win?

LEG FACT
Insects have six legs. Spiders have eight.

FACT
Black widow spiders are venomous, but only the female's bite can be dangerous to humans. Venom is a kind of poison.

ROUND 1

BLACK WIDOW SPIDER VS. DRAGONFLY

MATCH 1

The dragonfly is soaring around. It flies close to the web of a black widow spider.

FUN FACT
Dragonflies have four wings. They can fly forward and backward, and they can hover.

DID YOU KNOW?
There are thousands of different species of dragonflies.

BONUS FACT
A dragonfly has six legs but it can't walk.

BLACK WIDOW SPIDER WINS!

The tip of the dragonfly's wing gets caught in the web of the spider. The black widow has bad eyesight, but it feels the vibrations of the trapped dragonfly.

FUN FACT
Spiders are not insects. Spiders are arachnids.

IDENTI-FACT
Dragonflies are easy to recognize. They have long bodies and see-through wings.

As the dragonfly tries to free itself, the black widow attacks. The spider bites the dragonfly and injects it with deadly venom. The dragonfly will be dinner.

A centipede has no wings and cannot fly, but it is good at walking. The centipede sees an assassin bug. This could be trouble.

DID YOU KNOW?
The name centipede means "one hundred feet." A centipede doesn't really have one hundred feet. It has between thirty and three hundred.

ROUND 1

CENTIPEDE VS. ASSASSIN BUG

MATCH 2

The centipede is scary looking. Will the assassin bug just run away? No! The assassin bug faces the oncoming centipede.

FACT
Assassin bugs stab other insects with their long mouthparts and suck out their insides.

KISSING FACT
Assassin bugs are also called kissing bugs. They sometimes bite humans on the face near the lips.

CENTIPEDE WINS!

At first, the assassin bug is aggressive. But the flexible centipede moves its body quickly and uses its multiple legs to pin the assassin bug.

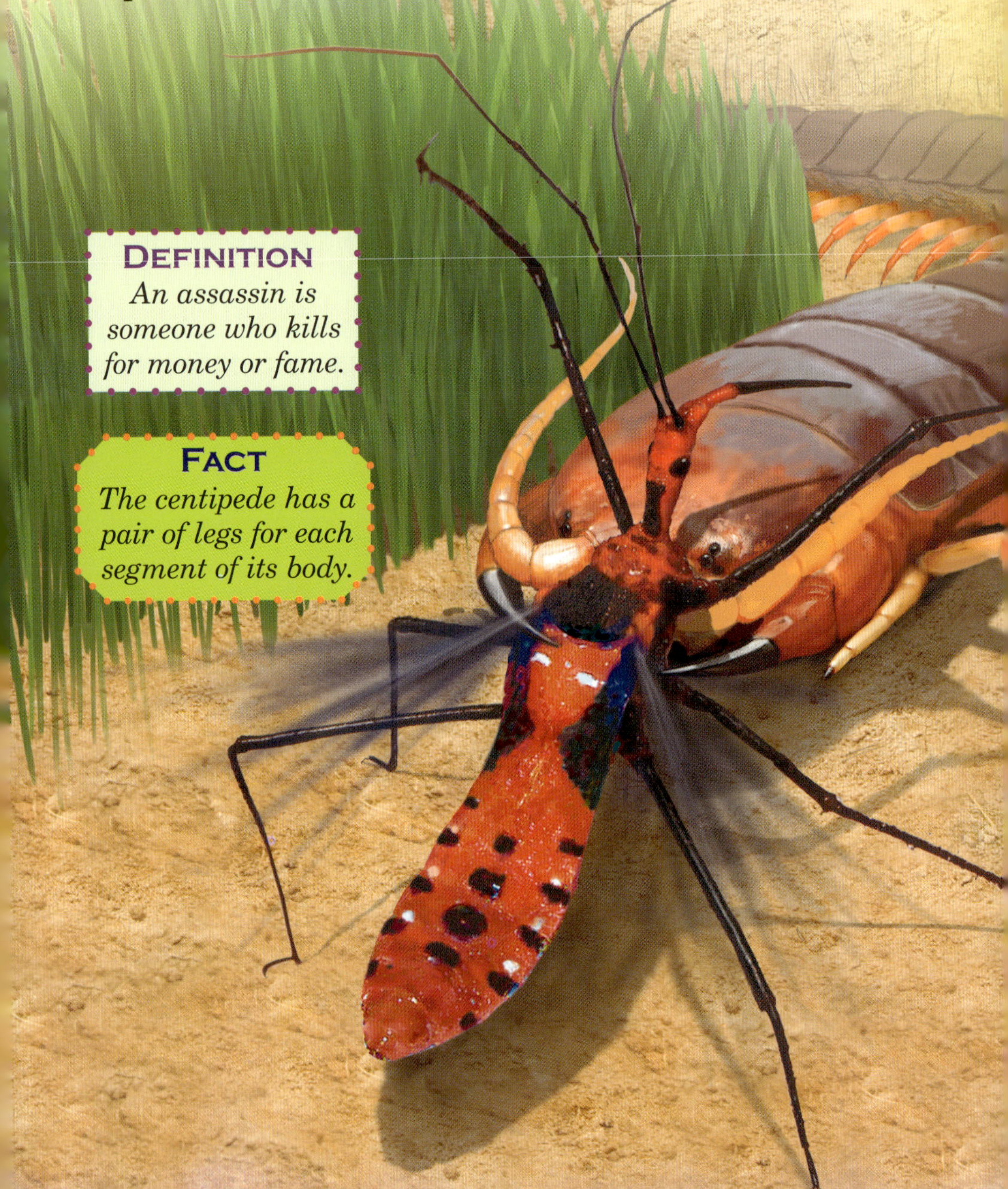

DEFINITION

An assassin is someone who kills for money or fame.

FACT

The centipede has a pair of legs for each segment of its body.

One! Two! Three! The centipede bites a chunk out of the assassin bug. The centipede will go on to fight the black widow spider.

A butterfly? What are you doing in this competition? You should be in a beauty contest, not a fight.

FUN FACT
Butterflies have no teeth, no claws, and no stingers.

FACT
Butterflies have scales on their wings. They look like small shingles.

ROUND 1

BUTTERFLY VS. KILLER BEE

MATCH 3

This unusual matchup has a colorful flier versus a dangerous stinging insect.

FIGHTING FACT
Killer bees are aggressive honeybees.

HYBRID FACT
Killer bees are a crossbreed of the African honeybee and the European honeybee.

KILLER BEE WINS!

The butterfly flies around, trying to confuse the killer bee. The killer bee heads straight for the butterfly and stings it in the head. The butterfly stops flying and crashes. It dies.

FACT
A butterfly's best defense is to fly away.

STINGING FACT
A swarm of killer bees could kill almost any animal. People must avoid killer bees.

DEFINITION
A swarm is a dense group of flying insects.

Bees can sting a human only once. They can sting soft insects multiple times. The killer bee moves on to the second round.

The spiky front legs of a praying mantis are designed to catch prey. This insect normally eats whatever it can catch. The praying mantis turns its head and sees a cockroach.

BEHAVIOR FACT
A praying mantis is an ambush predator. It lies in wait to catch prey.

ROUND 1

PRAYING MANTIS VS. COCKROACH

MATCH 4

Watch out, praying mantis. The cockroach is a tough pest. It can live for weeks without food. Some can run up to three miles per hour. That's fast for an insect.

FACT
Cockroach antennae look like loose strings.

WING FACT
Cockroach wings overlap. Beetle wings fold neatly in a straight line.

cockroach **beetle**

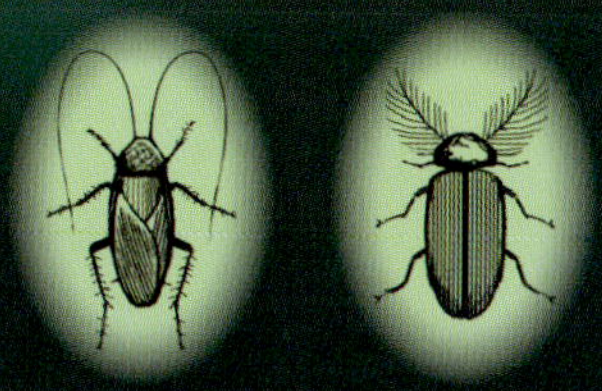

PRAYING MANTIS WINS!

This is not a quick fight. The praying mantis goes after the cockroach. The cockroach runs away. The praying mantis pursues and corners it.

FACT
Cockroaches are found from the Arctic to the tropics and in every type of environment.

DID YOU KNOW?
Some people keep praying mantises as pets.

The cockroach tries to fly, but the praying mantis hooks it with its front legs and damages it.

Crunch! Crunch! Bite! The praying mantis wins.

The next contest pairs a hornet with a tiger beetle. The hornet is hungry. It sees the tiger beetle.

DID YOU KNOW?
A word used by some people to describe a hornet is "nasty."

FACT
Hornets have stingers. They can sting multiple times.

ROUND 1

HORNET VS. TIGER BEETLE

MATCH 5

The tiger beetle prefers to walk, but it has wings and can fly. These two insects are on a collision course.

FUN FACT
There are hundreds of thousands of different species of beetles. They are one of the most successful life-forms on earth.

FACT
Beetles are biters.

HORNET WINS!

The aggressive hornet flies right at the tiger beetle. The tiger beetle fights back. After one sting, the tiger beetle thinks it's best to fly away. Now both insects are airborne, flying in circles, trying to attack each other.

FACT
A hornet is in the wasp family of insects.

VISION FACT
A tiger beetle cannot see while running.

The hornet can maneuver better in the air. It stings the tiger beetle several times. It gets harder for the wounded beetle to fly. The hornet wins and flies on to the second round.

RUMBLE UPDATE: Five matches down, three to go.

The daddy longlegs enters the competition. It is tall and skinny. It may be wondering if entering this contest was a good idea.

BODY-TYPE FACT
Look! It only has one body part. The head, thorax, and abdomen are all one.

FUN FACT
The daddy longlegs has eight legs but it is not a spider. It is in an order called harvestmen.

ROUND 1

DADDY LONGLEGS VS. SCORPION

MATCH 6

A scorpion is loaded with weapons: pincers, a biting mouth, and a stinging tail.

DID YOU KNOW?
A false scorpion looks identical to a scorpion, but it has no stinger.

SCORPION WINS!

The daddy longlegs ignores the scorpion and walks right over it. The daddy longlegs is so light, the scorpion hardly feels it.

FACT
A fossilized daddy longlegs proved to be about four hundred million years old. As a species, it knows how to survive.

DID YOU KNOW?
The daddy longlegs has only one pair of eyes.

The battle begins. The scorpion has too much firepower. Sting! Pinch! Sting! Pinch! The stinging scorpion wins! Aren't we humans lucky a scorpion isn't as big as a pickup truck?

If you touch or squeeze a stinkbug, it stinks. However, some people don't mind how these bugs smell.

YUMMY FACT
Some people eat stinkbugs. They say the bugs taste like apples. Yum!

ROUND 1 STINKBUG VS. WOOLLY BEAR MATCH 7

Should a gentle caterpillar be in this book? Oh well! The fight is on.

FACT
A caterpillar is the larva of a butterfly or a moth. This woolly bear is a tiger moth.

DEFINITION
The larval stage is the immature stage of an insect's life.

FACT
Some woolly bears are blond.

WOOLLY BEAR WINS!

The woolly bear coughs up some slime, which smells awful. Even the stinkbug doesn't like it. The two bugs meet! The woolly bear refuses to fight and rolls itself into a ball.

FACT
Stinkbugs are in a class of insects known as "true bugs."

Suddenly a bird swoops in and eats the stinkbug. The woolly bear caterpillar wins by accident, which sometimes happens in the animal kingdom.

The crowd is chanting! "Fuzzy! Fuzzy! Fuzzy!" It sounds like the fuzzy woolly bear may be a fan favorite!

Our last match of the first round is a noisy cicada versus a big hairy spider. Welcome the tarantula, our sixteenth contestant.

SHEDDING FACT
Both of these creatures shed their skin, which is called molting.

STRANGE FACT
Some cicadas come out of the ground only once, after seventeen years, then die five to six weeks later.

ROUND 1

CICADA VS. TARANTULA

MATCH 8

FACT
The tarantula has eight legs. The two long appendages next to its mouth are called palps.

OLD-AGE FACT
Some tarantulas live up to thirty years. Cicadas live for less than six weeks.

The tarantula gets annoyed listening to the cicada, the loudest insect in the world.

TARANTULA WINS!

This is a mismatch. Wham! The heavy tarantula jumps on the cicada and sinks its fangs in. The cicada stops singing.

FACT
A cicada makes noise by vibrating its bumpy exoskeleton.

DEFINITION
Bugs do not have bones. They have an exoskeleton, which is an exterior shell.

On to the second round!

Welcome to round two. We have the black widow spider fighting the centipede. Insects have six legs, so neither of these bugs is an insect.

SCIENTIFIC FACT
The creatures in this book are called invertebrates. *None has a backbone.*

FACT
There is an old video game called Centipede.

ROUND 2 BLACK WIDOW SPIDER VS. CENTIPEDE MATCH 1

The centipede may be the most surprising of all the contestants. No one expected it to get this far.

SLANG FACT
It's okay to call all the creatures in this book bugs. "Bug" is an acceptable slang term for spiders, insects, and other invertebrates.

CENTIPEDE WINS!

The centipede is overpowering. The black widow spider tries to bite, but its tender body can't handle the weight and shiftiness of all those centipede legs.

DANGER!
If you get bitten by a black widow, go to the hospital right away.

NUMBER FACT
A group of bugs similar to centipedes are called millipedes. Millipede means "one thousand feet."

The black widow is on top, then the centipede is on top. The fight goes back and forth.

Bite! The centipede wins. Sorry, black widow. You lost.

The killer bee returns for round two. It has a nasty look. Other bugs should beware! It will fight the praying mantis. The fans can't wait!

FACT
Killer bees in Asia have figured out how to kill a giant hornet.

ROUND 2

KILLER BEE VS. PRAYING MANTIS

MATCH 2

The praying mantis has quick reflexes. The killer bee is a better flier. Usually only male praying mantises can fly.

FACT
A praying mantis can turn its triangle-shaped head backward.

PRAYING MANTIS WINS!

The killer bee tries to sting the praying mantis. But the praying mantis is too quick. Its strong arms grab the killer bee out of the air. The bee tries a spin-and-sting move.

KNEELING FACT

The praying mantis got its name because its front legs make it look like it is kneeling in worship.

The praying mantis bites first, which ends the fight quickly. The praying mantis moves on to the next round. The killer bee did not live up to its name.

This match is bad attitude versus more bad attitude. Flying stinger versus stinger and pincers. Six legs versus eight legs.

DID YOU KNOW?
The biggest hornet in the world is the Asian giant hornet.

ROUND 2

HORNET VS. SCORPION

MATCH 3

FACT
One of the deadliest scorpions is known as a deathstalker.

This matchup is everything an Ultimate Bug Rumble fan could want.

HORNET WINS!

The hornet avoids the scorpion's strength by attacking from above. Seeing an opening, the hornet stings the scorpion and flies away. Ouch! It sees another opportunity and stings again. Ouch!

POISON FACT
Both hornets and scorpions have venom in their stingers.

SHARP FACT
Hornets and scorpions can sting multiple times.

A couple more stings, and the scorpion is badly hurt. It loses strength. The hornet's strategy works. Scorpions can't fly, so airpower wins!

Fuzzy! Fuzzy! Fuzzy! This fan favorite is back for round two. It's fuzzy versus hairy.

DID YOU KNOW?
The woolly bear has thirteen body segments.

FACT
Caterpillars have only six legs, although it looks like they have more. They are insects.

ROUND 2

WOOLLY BEAR VS. TARANTULA

MATCH 4

It looks like the tarantula will have an easy opponent.

FACT
There are almost 1,000 different species of tarantulas. Maybe some live in your neighborhood.

TARANTULA WINS!

The woolly bear rolls itself into a ball. The tarantula is not fooled.

NICKNAME
The woolly bear is also called the black-ended bear or the woolly worm.

The tarantula pounces on the woolly bear. The tarantula sinks its fangs in. Fuzzy lost.

Round two is over. Centipede, praying mantis, hornet, and tarantula are heading to the semifinal round, which we'll call the "Bug Four"!

The second round is over. Welcome to the third round, or Bug Four. It has been an exciting single-elimination fight. Get ready for the multilegged centipede to fight the bug-eating praying mantis.

FACT
The largest centipede in the world is the Amazonian giant centipede.

50/50 FACT
Half of the Bug Four are insects.

ROUND 3

CENTIPEDE VS. PRAYING MANTIS

MATCH 1

The fans will be watching all of those legs. The praying mantis has six. It looks like the centipede has a million.

OCEAN FACT
A mantis shrimp has the same snatching arms as a praying mantis.

PRAYING MANTIS WINS!

The centipede crawls over the praying mantis. It tries to bite but the praying mantis flies away. Every time the centipede gets close, the praying mantis seems to escape.

EXPENSIVE FACT

Aren't you glad you don't have to buy shoes for the centipede?

The praying mantis bites one leg off the centipede, then another. After removing a few more legs, the praying mantis delivers a fatal bite. Praying mantis, you are going to the finals!

It's the hornet versus the tarantula. This fight may not be fair. The hornet has already defeated the tiger beetle and the scorpion.

FINALS FACT
There can be only one Ultimate Bug Rumble champion!

ROUND 3 HORNET VS. TARANTULA MATCH 2

The tarantula has big fangs, but it has no wings. The tarantula has defeated the cicada and the woolly bear. Who will get to the finals?

HORNET WINS!

The hornet wastes no time. It buzzes toward the tarantula's face. The tarantula gets up on its hind legs and tries boxing. It misses. The hornet flies in circles and does a loop-the-loop. The hornet then stings the tarantula

The hornet keeps stinging it. It stings so many times, th tarantula stops walking and collapses. The hornet flies o to the final match.

CHAMPIONSHIP MATCH!

It's the final fight of the tournament: praying mantis versus hornet. The praying mantis flies, then tries to snatch and bite off the hornet's head. The hornet buzzes away.

CHAMPIONSHIP FACT

This competition started with sixteen bugs.

The fight goes airborne! The heavily armed hornet is too quick. It stings the praying mantis multiple times. These two insects fight back and forth. The mantis is usually a great fighter, but the smaller, faster hornet is more aggressive.

HORNET WINS!

Just as the praying mantis thinks it has the hornet in its grasp, the hornet outmaneuvers the praying mantis. With a sting, sting, sting, the praying mantis falls over. Too much firepower. The hornet wins!

This is one way the competition might have ended. Write your own ending or think of a new version of an Ultimate Rumble book.